CH-47 Chinook

Written by David Doyle

In Action®

CH47D

UNITED STATES ARMY

Squadron Signal
Publications

Line Illustrations by Vincenzo Auletta

(Front Cover) A CH-47A from the "Long Horns," B Company, 228th Assault Support Helicopter Battalion (ASHB), 1st Cavalry Division, unloads troops from C Company, 1st Battalion, 50th Mech at Landing Zone (LZ) Quick, where they are beginning a search-and-destroy mission in the Cây Giếp Mountains, Bình Định Province, Vietnam, in October 1967. (National Archives)

(Back Cover) Two CH-47F Chinooks from Company H, 1st Battalion, 214th Aviation Regiment, 12th Combat Aviation Brigade, take off to pick up air-assault troops during NATO Exercise Trident Juncture 2015, in Zaragoza, Spain, on 3 November 2015. (DVIDS)

About the In Action® Series

In Action® books, despite the title of the genre, are books that trace the development of a single type of aircraft, armored vehicle, or ship from prototype to the final production variant. Experimental or "one-off" variants can also be included. Our first *In Action*® book was printed in 1971.

ISBN 978-0-89747-841-0

 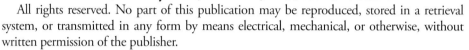

Proudly printed in the U.S.A.
Copyright 2017 Squadron/Signal Publications
1115 Crowley Drive, Carrollton, TX 75006-1312 U.S.A.

Military/Combat Photographs and Snapshots

If you have any photos of aircraft, armor, soldiers, or ships of any nation, particularly wartime snapshots, please share them with us and help make Squadron/Signal's books all the more interesting and complete in the future. Any photograph sent to us will be copied and returned as requested. Electronic images are preferred. The donor will be fully credited for any photos used. Please send them to:

Squadron/Signal Publications
1115 Crowley Drive
Carrollton, TX 75006-1312 U.S.A.
www.Squadron.com

(Title Page) From the early 1960s to the present, the CH-47 Chinook has been a constant in the U.S. Army, transporting men, supplies, and equipment wherever and whenever needed. In this undated photograph, a CH-47D, serving as a test aircraft, is airlifting an M198 155mm howitzer, weighing approximately 15,800 pounds. (National Archives)

Acknowledgements

This book was completed with the considerable help of my friends Tom Kailbourn, Jim Gilmore, Dana Bell, Sean Hert, and Bob Steinbrunn. The resources of the National Archives, Army Aviation Museum, and San Diego Air and Space Museum provided many of the images. Those images without other credit are from Defense Visual Information Center. Neither this book, nor any of the others, could have been completed without the ongoing help and support of my darling wife Denise.

Introduction

With its tandem, contra-rotating rotors whirling above an aluminum fuselage punctuated by round porthole windows, the CH-47 Chinook heavy-lift helicopter has become something of an icon – a status it owes in no small part to its long service life of already more than 55 years – a career that some experts predict will ultimately reach a century of service.

While conventional helicopters require a torque-counteracting tail rotor that consumes 15% of engine power, tandem-rotor choppers put all the engine power into lift. The price for this increase in power is a substantially more complicated transmission and control system.

The U.S. military has been interested in tandem-rotor helicopters at least since the 1947 XR-11 Dragonfly. However, it was engineer Frank N. Piasecki, then heading Piasecki Helicopter Corporation, that made the tandem-rotor helicopter viable for military use. Beginning with the PV-3 (HRP-2) Harp, popularly known as the "Flying Banana," Piasecki Helicopter Corporation supplied the military with an array of tandem-rotor helicopters, including the XHJP-1, later designated the HUP-1 Mule and the H-21 "Shawnee." By 1957 the firm no longer employed Piasecki, and when the H-21 arrived in Vietnam in December 1961 to become the first U.S. tandem-rotor chopper to see combat, its manufacturer – now known as Vertol Aircraft Corporation – had begun work on a new, turbine-powered tandem-rotor aircraft: the V-107.

Nearly a decade before the Boeing CH-47, Sikorsky introduced its H-34. Powered by a piston engine, the H-34 ably served the U.S. Army, Navy, and Marines as a military heavy-lift helicopter from the mid-1950s through the Vietnam War. (National Archives)

One of the first large helicopters, the Piasecki H-16 was nearly the size of a DC-4 transport, and could carry 47 men. Only two of the H-16 tandem-rotor aircraft were built, with the first flight occurring on 23 October 1953. The program was cancelled after the second prototype crashed on 5 January 1956, killing the two crewmen. (National Archives)

First flying in 1952, the Piasecki H-21 was a tandem-rotor transport chopper used by the U.S. Army and U.S. Air Force. Dubbed the "Flying Banana" because of its shape, it was well suited to operations in extreme cold. The H-21 was the mainstay of the Army's heavy lift helicopter operations until the advent of the CH-47 Chinook. (National Archives)

3

Development

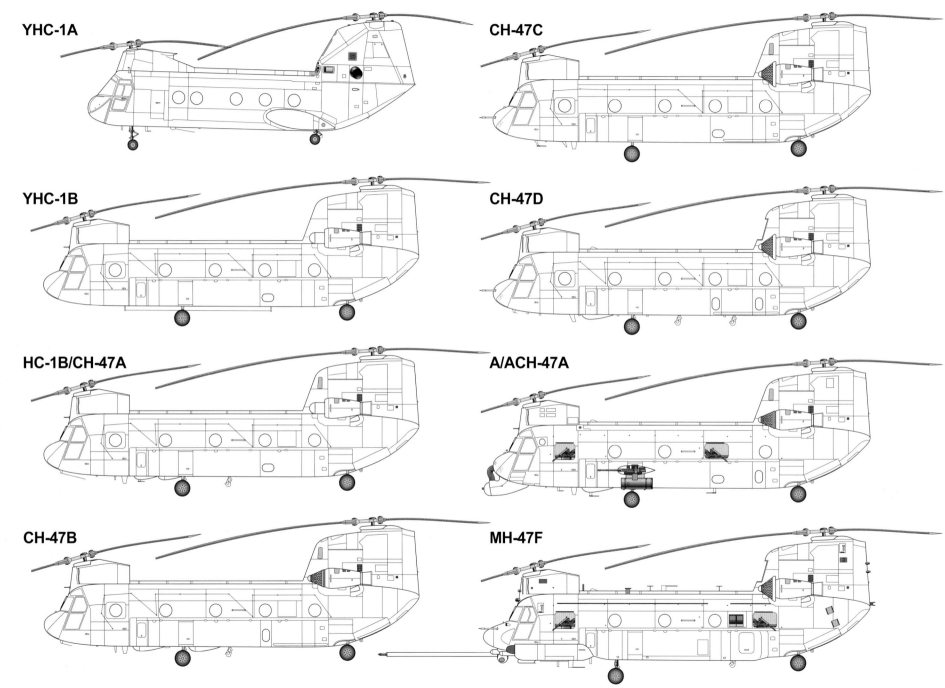

YHC-1A

YHC-1B

HC-1B/CH-47A

CH-47B

CH-47C

CH-47D

A/ACH-47A

MH-47F

In the mid-1950s, Vertol Aircraft conducted a study of the American military's future needs for cargo helicopters. The concept of air-mobility was coming to the fore in military thinking, and the Army desired a helicopter with the same carrying capabilities as a standard 2½-ton truck. Based on those findings, Vertol undertook privately the design and development of a medium-lift helicopter with tandem rotors, an aircraft that the company designated Model BV-107. The twin General Electric YT58-GE-6 turbine engines were housed in the rear rotor pylon. The Army received three prototypes in 1957, designating them YHC-1A, one of which is seen here in a May 1960 photo, by which time Vertol had merged with Boeing and been renamed Boeing Vertol. (National Archives)

The Boeing Vertol YHC-1A had a tricycle landing gear, as seen in this frontal view at Fort Benning, Georgia, in May 1960. These prototypes were powered by General Electric YT58-GE-6 engines, and the fuselages were watertight, for landings on water. (National Archives)

The YHC-1A had a spacious interior, with folding seats for passengers. A man is seated in the forward right folding seat. There were an uninterrupted floor, sidewalls, and ceiling in the cargo compartment for the easy loading of men, vehicles, and cargo. (National Archives)

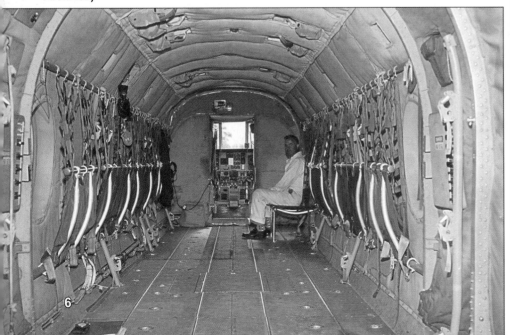

To permit easy boarding and egress for troops, cargo, and vehicles, a rear ramp was a feature of the Boeing Vertol YHC-1A. The two rotor pylons were tall, in order to cut down on the amount of dust the rotors churned up when on or near the ground. (National Archives)

The Boeing Vertol 107-II was a civilian and export version of the Model YHC-1A. This example, which displays corporate livery, with square windows for the passengers, is landing at the Pentagon's helipad. Its civil registration number was N6674D. (National Archives)

The first of the three Boeing Vertol YHC-1As was assigned U.S. Army serial number 58-5514 and tail number 85514. In 1962 these prototypes were redesignated YCH-46C. They served as the basis for the CH-46 Sea Knight helicopters. (Army Aviation Museum)

The Vertol V-107 was born from a company-initiated study of what the U.S. military would want in a twin-turbine helicopter. Thomas Pepper, Chief of Preliminary Design for Vertol, spoke to a number of Army experts in air mobility, and found that what the Army wanted was essentially a flying 2½-ton truck. The initial Army interviews were followed by additional, detailed interviews with Marine, Navy, NACA, as well as Army personnel. These interviews yielded a framework of specifications for a rear loading, easily maintainable, and easily retrofitted helicopter with high-mounted engines (protecting the engines from foreign objects and ground personnel from exhaust and noise), suitable for carrier operations and permitting indiscriminate loading of personnel or cargo.

Vertol designers studied no fewer than 300 possible configurations before settling on what they dubbed their Model 107. On 22 July 1957, the company presented the Army a three-step plan for the creation of the Model 107. This plan was in part conditioned on the Army loaning to Vertol engines for use in the prototype, and the right to use the information gained from the construction and testing of the prototype toward development of a new medium-transport helicopter.

The prototype was rolled out on 31 March 1958, with the first flight lifting off from Philadelphia International Airport on 22 April 1958. The military designation for the Model 107 was the YHC-1. The contract initially called for the construction of 10 YHC-1 helicopters, but after an initial review, the Army felt that the Model 107 was too small for a transport aircraft, and too large for an assault helicopter. An enlarged version, Model 114, which will be discussed later, was designed and designated the YHC-1B, and the model 107 became the YHC-1A. While the Army ardently pursued further development of the YHC-1B, the Navy and Marine Corps opted for the smaller YHC-1A, which became the CH-46 Sea Knight.

The Vertol Model 107 was adopted by the Navy and the Marine Corps as the CH-46, and served the Corps from 1961 through 2015, when it was finally retired. Here, a Helicopter Combat Support Squadron 8 (HC-8) CH-46 Sea Knight helicopter takes off from the helicopter pad of the ammunition ship USS *Mount Baker* (AE-34) in the Caribbean in 1988.

The Army decided that it required a larger medium-lift helicopter than the YHC-1A, so in May 1959 it ordered five YHC-1B service-test prototypes. These differed from the YHC-1A in that they had a longer fuselage, quadricycle rather than tricycle landing gear, and turbine engines in external pods rather than housed in the aft rotor pylon. In addition, the YHC-1B had a long sponson or pod on each side of the lower part of the fuselage that housed the fuel tanks, electronics equipment, and supports for the landing gear. Shown here is the fourth YHC-1B, registration number 59-4985. At the time, the rotors were not installed, but Vertol touched-in the rotors when they sent this photo to the Army. The YHC-1B would prove to be the basis for the CH-47 Chinook helicopter. (National Archives)

On 25 June 1958, the Army issued an invitation for a General Management Proposal for the U.S. Army Medium Transport Helicopter program, which was intended to produce a replacement for the CH-21, CH-34, and CH-37.

Five firms – Bell, Kaman, McDonnell, Sikorsky and Vertol – responded with proposals for what was known as Weapon System SS471L. Vertol offered several engine options, including a three-engine/four-rotor-blade Lycoming T-55 L3 (1,250 shaft horse power [s.h.p.] each) configuration, four GE T64-GE8 engines (1,250 s.h.p. each) scenario or two GE T64-GE2 (2,650 s.h.p. each) design. With the T-55 configuration, the aircraft was expected to have four-bladed, 59-ft. rotors, gross 33,703 pounds, and be capable of a maximum speed of 150 knots.

On 4 March 1959, the Joint Army/Air Force Source Selection Board recommended that Vertol be awarded the management contract for the medium-transport helicopter. Due to Army funding problems, the Air Force was asked to negotiate a development contract for the new aircraft (which Vertol designated the Model 114). The $19 million contract, awarded in June 1959, was for engineering, tooling, five airframes, a mock-up, and initial testing of the Model 114, which bore the military designation YHC-1B.

Because of changes in the design gross weight, reset at 33,000 pounds, only two Lycoming T-55-L5 turbo-shaft engines rated at 1,940 s.h.p. each, turning two three-bladed rotors, were required. The overall fuselage length was established as 51 feet.

On 16 November 1959, Vertol and Boeing announced that Boeing was seeking to acquire Vertol, and on 31 March 1960 Vertol became a division of Boeing.

YHC-1B serial number 59-4985 appears with only the forward rotor installed. The photo was taken to document the ability of the helicopter's ramp and cargo compartment to accommodate a truck as large as the Dodge M37 ¾-ton truck.

Still lacking its aft rotor, Boeing Vertol YHC-1B registration number 59-4985 is viewed from the right side. These service-test YHC-1Bs had a capacity of 10,100 pounds of internal cargo or 16,000 pounds of external cargo. For the purposes of external cargo, the helicopter was equipped with a winch-operated 16,000-pound cargo hook on the belly. Folding seats were included in the cargo compartment for 33 troops, compared with 22 passengers in the YHC-1A.

The second Boeing Vertol YHC-1B service-test helicopter, registration number 59-4983, shown during a test flight on 19 October 1961, was the first Chinook helicopter to fly, making its maiden flight on 21 September 1961, with Boeing Vertol test pilot Leonard La Vassar at the controls. The U.S. Army accepted this helicopter on 24 April 1964, and it served until stricken from the rolls on 1 March 1970. (National Archives)

Boeing Vertol YHC-1B registration number 59-4983 hovers during a test on 19 October 1961. This helicopter had a paint scheme of glossy white with high-visibility orange. A long air-data probe, also called a test boom, is mounted on the nose. (National Archives)

The same helicopter shown in the two preceding photos, Boeing Vertol YHC-1B serial number 59-4983, is viewed from the right side during tests on 19 October 1961. Escape hatches were outlined for rescue workers' ease of identification. (National Archives)

11

A Boeing Vertol YHC-1B, presumably serial number 59-4983, hovers feet above the ground in front of a hangar. A star-and-bars national insignia is on its belly. Parked on the hardstand in front of the hangar are several Boeing Vertol 107-II helicopters, while another YHC-1B is in the hangar. The extensions seen on the tops of the rotor hubs would not be features on the production CH-47 Chinooks. (National Archives)

Based on the YHC-1B with some upgrades, the CH-47A Chinook helicopter went into production. It was powered by two Lycoming T55-L-7 engines, rated at 2,650 shaft horsepower each. The Army designated the CH-47A as its official medium helicopter in October 1963, and a total of 349 were completed. The third production CH-47A, serial number 60-3450, was the first one to be delivered to the U.S. Army, and is seen here during a static-line paratrooper jump exercise. (National Archives)

The fourth CH-47A Chinook, serial number 60-3451, is parked in a field while assisting in the transport of a missile battery. A large part of the Chinook's mission as envisioned by the Army was the rapid movement of artillery from one emplacement to another. (Army Aviation Museum)

Using the high-capacity hook on the belly, CH-47A, serial number 62-2119, transports a slung M56 Scorpion 90mm self-propelled gun into a simulated combat area during training maneuvers at Fort Benning, Georgia, on 10 July 1964. (National Archives)

In 1963, CH-47A 61-2425 airlifts a 6x6 cargo truck at McCoy Air Force Base, Florida, during an evaluation of the Chinook's ability to rapidly move missile batteries – "shoot-and-scoot" – to establish a new emplacement before the enemy can hit back. (Army Aviation Museum)

Rotors folded for storage, U.S. Army CH-47A Chinook medium helicopter is viewed close-up from the front left at Fort Sill, Oklahoma, in October 1966. On the nose adjacent to the pilot's and copilot's lower windows are communications antennas. A panel marked "ACCESS" is between the antennas. On the sides of the fuselage were short mounting posts, called "standoffs," on which high-frequency wire antennas could be affixed. (National Archives)

CH-47A 66-0066 at Fort Sill, Oklahoma, in October 1966. Jutting below the chin of the helicopter, and also visible in the preceding photo, is a rear-view mirror, with which the pilot and copilot could observe the operation of the cargo hook. This mirror later was omitted when the crew chief was tasked with monitoring the cargo hook. Toward the front of the fuselage pod is the open access hatch for the electronics compartment. (National Archives)

The engine pods of early- and late-production CH-47A Chinooks are compared in these diagrams. The late-production CH-47As had a conical screen over the engine intake to keep out foreign objects. The screen did not diminish engine performance. (National Archives)

A tow tractor is hitched to the rear of CH-47 66-0066 at Fort Sill on 17 October 1966. The front landing gear had dual wheels, while the rear gears had single wheels. On top of the fuselage is a framework made of pipes, to support the folded rotor blades. (National Archives)

**CH-47A
(Early)**

**CH-47A
(Late)**

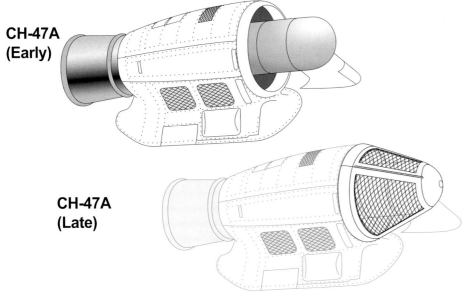

ACH-47A

As helicopter-borne infantry tactics were refined during the Vietnam war, the need for heavily armed and armored support helicopters became apparent. Seeking something heavier than the AH-1G Cobra, the Army turned to Boeing Vertol. On 23 June 1965 the company proposed creating the ACH-47A gunship. A contract was signed on 30 June 1965, and the next week work began on the first example, serial number 64-13145.

The aircraft first flew on 6 November 1965 and was delivered to the Army the next month. It was soon joined by three additional production ACH-47A aircraft.

Each ACH-47A carried five M60D 7.62x51mm machine guns or M2HB .50-caliber machine guns, two M24A1 20mm cannons mounted on stub wings, fed with 800 rounds of ammo. Also on the stub wings were shackles for holding two XM159B/XM159C 19-Tube 2.75" rocket launchers or two M18/M18A1 7.62x51mm gun pods. There was a single XM5 40mm grenade launcher in a turret under the nose. Five hundred rounds of ammunition were supplied for the XM5.

Three of the four aircraft, 64-13149 "Easy Money," 64-13151 "Stump Jumper," and 64-13154, "Birth Control" deployed to Vung Tau, Vietnam in June 1966, designated as the 53rd Aviation Detachment (Provisional), 1st Cavalry Division. "Co$t of Living," 64-13145, initially remained stateside. After "Stump Jumper" was lost in a taxi accident in August 1966, "Co$t of Living" went overseas as well. This ACH-47A shot itself down in May 1967 when a cannon mounting pin failed, and all eight crewmembers perished. "Birth Control" was shot down in February 1968, and while the crew of "Easy Money" rescued the personnel, the gunship was lost. Because tactics required the aircraft operate in pairs, "Easy Money" was withdrawn from service, and is today preserved in Alabama.

One of the ACH-47As is seen from the left side during a hover. Light-colored horizontal bars are aft of the machine-gun windows, while a large, vertical bar is on the aft rotor pylon. The prominent chin turret made the ACH-47As unmistakable in profile. (Army Aviation Museum)

Based on early experience of helicopter operations in Vietnam, the Army Materiel Command, Aberdeen, Maryland, proposed an armed and armored version of the CH-47, capable of suppressing enemy fire and defeating small-arms fire at landing zones. This helicopter was designated ACH-47A, and Boeing Vertol converted four CH-47As to these gunships in late 1965. Two of them are shown here, showing their M5 chin turrets with M75 40mm grenade launcher and right stub wing with an M24A1 20mm cannon and rocket pod. (Army Aviation Museum)

An XM159 2.75-inch rocket pod is viewed close-up without the 19 rockets loaded. The pods were mounted on pylons attached to the stub wings. Details of the M24A1 20mm cannon are also visible, as are its ammo feed and cartridge-ejector chute. (Army Aviation Museum)

Colonel John Harland Swenson, U.S. Army, stands next to an ACH-47A, with armament on the right stub wing consisting of an M24A1 20mm cannon over a General Electric M18E1 7.62mm Minigun, a pod-contained rotary gun and 1,500 rounds of ammunition. (Army Aviation Museum)

These diagrams show the weapons installed in the ACH-47A, including window-mounted .50-caliber machine guns, a .50-caliber machine-gun and ammunition-box installation on the lowered ramp, and the choice of weapons that the helicopter could carry on its stub wings.

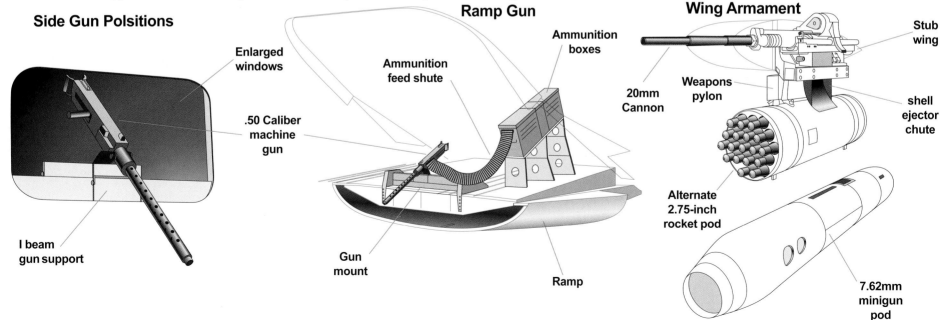

Side Gun Polsitions

Enlarged windows

.50 Caliber machine gun

I beam gun support

Ramp Gun

Ammunition feed shute

Ammunition boxes

Gun mount

Ramp

Wing Armament

Stub wing

20mm Cannon

Weapons pylon

shell ejector chute

Alternate 2.75-inch rocket pod

7.62mm minigun pod

18

In collaboration with the U.S. Army, Boeing Vertol commenced work on an experimental helicopter based on the CH-47 in January 1969. Designated the Model 347, this helicopter had a longer fuselage than the CH-47, in addition to having four-bladed rotors and a 45-foot wing. For this project, the Army lent to Boeing Vertol a CH-47A, registration number 65-7992. The Model 347 made its first flight on 27 May 1970. (San Diego Air and Space Museum)

The extended fuselage of the Boeing Vertol Model 347 is apparent in this photo from the left side. The wings, installed after the initial flight tests, acted to unload the rotors, and had variable incidence and full-span flaps. The one-off Model 347 (also called the BV-347) was conceived to develop and test concepts and components for future heavy-lift helicopters. The fuselage was 9 feet, 2 inches longer than that of the CH-47. (Army Aviation Museum)

During the initial tests of the Boeing Vertol Model 347, the helicopter was fitted with fairings in the shoulder position, where the wings later would be mounted. The 347 was equipped with retractable landing gear. When retracted, the aft wheels remained exposed below the rear of the fuselage pylons, as seen in this photo of the helicopter in a low-level hover. Improvements to control noise and vibrations were incorporated in the Model 347. (Army Aviation Museum)

Following the Model 347 test program, that one-off aircraft, registration number 65-7992, was used for the testing of an advanced fly-by-wire flight-control system for a heavy-lift helicopter. "HLH FLY BY WIRE" was marked high up on the fuselage aft of the cockpit. (National Archives)

The fly-by-wire control system replaced the traditional hydro-mechanical connections from the flight controls to the rotors with electrical connections. A retractable gondola on the belly of the HLH Fly by Wire served as a control station for external loads. (National Archives)

The HLH Fly by Wire has a cargo container handler slung underneath during tests at Davison Army Airfield, Virginia, in 1974. This helicopter featured an automatic external load recovery system, enabling automated hover and cargo pickup. The rack-like container handler was designed to automatically lock onto the top of a cargo container, enabling rapid pickup and departure from the pickup site. (National Archives)

The fixture called the cargo container handler has locked on to a cargo container at Davison Army Airfield in 1974, and the HLH Fly by Wire aircraft has lifted the container. The rearward-facing operator in the gondola controlled the helicopter during lifting operations using a four-axis sidearm controller. Two lifting hooks were used, for better load stability, which also resulted in better flight stability. (National Archives)

In a final image of the HLH Fly by Wire aircraft conducting heavy-lifting tests at Davison Army Airfield in 1974, the load operator, positioned in the gondola, is wearing a helmet and is looking down toward the photographer. The gondola had clear panels on the sides and the floor, for better operator visibility. To the lower right is a cargo container with a container handler attached to it. (National Archives)

The CH-47B was an improved version of the CH-47A, with a stronger airframe and a higher-powered engine for better performance in the heat of Southeast Asia. This version was powered by two Lycoming T55-L-7C turbine engines rated at 2,850 shaft horsepower. Two key visual identifying features of the CH-47B compared with the -A model were a flat, rather than sharp, trailing edge for the aft rotor pylon, and strakes on the bottom rear of each fuselage sponson and on each side of the lower part of the ramp. Shown here is CH-47B serial number 67-18439, showing the ease with which it could lift a truck during a demonstration tour in Europe in 1967. (San Diego Air and Space Museum)

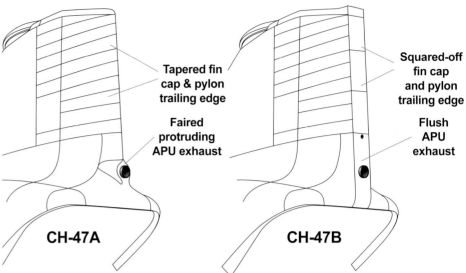

Tapered fin
cap & pylon
trailing edge

Faired
protruding
APU exhaust

Squared-off
fin cap
and pylon
trailing edge

Flush
APU
exhaust

CH-47A

CH-47B

A CH-47B accelerates away from a hover maneuver over an airfield during a 1967 demonstration tour in Europe. The left sponson strake may be seen from a point below the next-to-rear round window, to the rear of the sponson. (San Diego Air and Space Museum)

Civilian and military spectators watch a demonstration of a CH-47B at an air base in Europe in 1967. Faster and with greater range than the CH-47A, the CH-47B could lift heavier loads to greater altitudes in warm climates. (San Diego Air and Space Museum)

The aft rotor pylon of the CH-47A had a rounded top rear corner and a sharp trailing edge, while the aft rotor pylon of the CH-47B had a rounded upper rear corner and a flattened trailing edge. Differences in the APU exhausts also are illustrated.

For the CH-47B, and continuing in subsequent models of the Chinook, a strake was added toward the rear of each fuselage sponson and on each side of the lower part of the ramp. These modifications afforded better longitudinal stability during ramp-down flight operations.

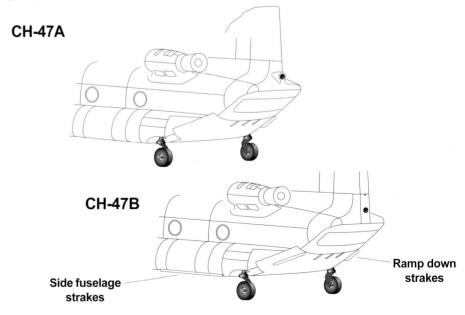

CH-47A

CH-47B

Side fuselage
strakes

Ramp down
strakes

The CH-47C was the result of an Army requirement for a helicopter that could transport a slung load of 15,000 pounds a distance of 30 nautical miles at 4,000 feet and in temperatures up to 95 degrees Fahrenheit. These requirements were satisfied with the help of two Lycoming T55-L-11C turboshaft engines rated at 3,750 shaft horse power (s.h.p.) each, coupled to 6,000 s.h.p. transmissions. In addition, the airframe was further strengthened, and the pitot tube on the front of the forward rotor pylon was deleted, and two new pitot tubes on extension posts were mounted on the nose. (National Archives)

While the CH-47A was well-received and successful, as is so often the case, there was a desire to increase performance. Toward this end, the first improved model was the CH-47B, which utilized T55-L-7C engines, each generating 2,850 shaft horse power (s.h.p.) and equipped with improved rotor blades with a steel main spar and honeycomb trailing edges, in lieu of the CH-47A's aluminum main spar and fiberglass trailing edges. These and other improvements boosted the maximum gross weight of the CH-47B to 33,000 pounds, a 4,500-pound increase over the CH-47A.

Despite the improvements brought about by the introduction of the B-model in 1967, that model remained in production for less than a year (10 May 1967 through 28 February 1968), before being superseded by the CH-47C. The CH-47C was the result of an effort to meet an Army requirement for increased range. In order to meet this requirement, engineers at Boeing Vertol, as Vertol had been renamed following the 31 March 1960 acquisition by the west-coast based aviation behemoth, increased the fuel capacity from the 621 gallons of the CH-47B to 1,100 gallons. During ferry flights, this capacity could be further augmented by adding four fuel bladders in the cargo compartment, increasing range to over 1,000 miles at 10,000 feet. This capability allowed the CH-47C to self-deploy to Europe, as was demonstrated in August 1979 by Operation Northern Leap, when Chinooks flew from Fort Carson, Colorado, to Heidelberg Army Air Field in Baden-Württemberg, Germany, with intermediate stops in Iowa, Pennsylvania, Maine, Canada, Greenland, Iceland, and England.

Later, both the CH-47B and the CH-47C were fitted with crash-resistant fuel tanks, that reduced their integral fuel capacities to 566 and 1,036 gallons respectively. The transmission was upgraded, as were the engines after a time. While the CH-47C initially used the 2,850-s.h.p. T55-L-7C engine, after production of 106 examples (subsequently dubbed the "Baby C"), the improved 3,750-s.h.p. T55-L-11 began to be installed. For a time, these aircraft were referred to as the "Super C." In time the Baby C aircraft were upgraded to Super C configuration.

In addition to the increased fuel capacity, several other improvements were marked by the introduction of the CH-47C. Among these are larger engine air intake dust and debris screens, an uprated drive shaft system, and dual automatic flight control and dual Stability Augmentation Systems vibration dampeners. During the course of production, new rotor blades, developed with the aid of NASA, began to be installed. The new high-lift cambered blades were made of steel, aluminum, and fiberglass.

The CH-47C began arriving in Vietnam in September 1968. There, the additional capabilities were quickly appreciated, especially the ability to lift heavy loads (up to 10,000 pounds) in the high elevations of the Central Highlands, where previous Chinooks had been restricted to 7,000 pounds.

Production of the CH-47C totaled 288 units, with 224 of these being delivered during the Vietnam War. Of the 166 CH-47C aircraft actually deployed in that conflict, 26 were lost due to enemy action or accidents. One of those was 67-18529, shot down on 16 February 1973 – three weeks AFTER the Paris Peace Accords were signed. The only casualty of the crash, and the last Army Aviation member killed in action in Vietnam, was SP5 James L. Scroggins, previously awarded the Distinguished Flying Cross for saving his crew.

The pitot tube on the front of the forward rotor pylon on the CH-47Bs was replaced on the CH-47Cs by a glide-slope antenna in that position, and a new pitot tube and two radar homing and warning (RHAW) antennas now were installed on the nose.

The dust and debris filters installed on CH-47Bs and retrofitted on some CH-47As were enlarged for the CH-47C, with the rear of the filter having a larger diameter than that of the engine intake. This configuration allowed for bypass air to exit the filter.

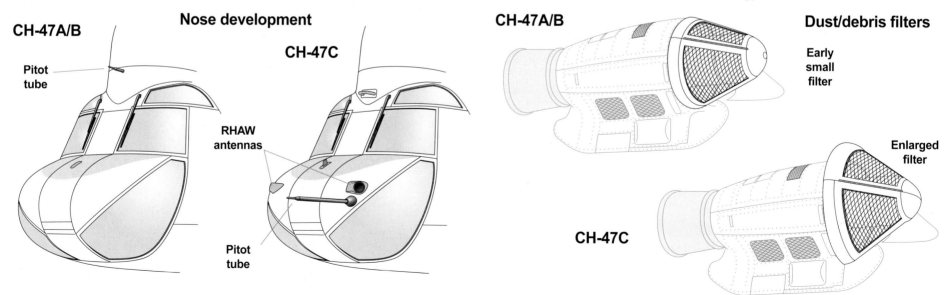

Nose development

CH-47A/B

Pitot tube

CH-47C

RHAW antennas

Pitot tube

CH-47A/B

Dust/debris filters

Early small filter

Enlarged filter

CH-47C

The CH-47D was intended as a Chinook with greater reliability, better maintainability, and more power than previous models. The program included new-construction CH-47Ds as well as earlier-model Chinooks upgraded to -D specifications. Some of the features included two Lycoming T55-L-712 turbine engines, three cargo hooks, a large opening in the front of the aft rotor pylon for oil-cooler ventilation, and two pitot tubes on the nose. In addition, the rotor blades, now fabricated from fiberglass, had a 32-inch chord, compared with 24 inches on the CH-47C. (Army Aviation Museum)

CH-47 MODERNIZATION PROGRAM

Much of the Army's inventory of Chinooks saw heavy use in the Vietnam War, with 577 aircraft, or 85% of the Chinooks built prior to 1973, being involved in the conflict. Of those, 141 were lost to accidents or enemy action, and those that survived showed obvious signs of heavy use. That use, while proving the soundness of the basic design, also pointed to some areas that were worthy of improvement.

A complete rebuild and modernization plan was devised that would involve stripping the airframe, repairing and renewing the airframe structure as needed, and then installing numerous improved components. So extensive was this work and modification that the resultant aircraft was given a new model number – the CH-47D. In addition, aircraft subjected to this process were given new serial numbers as well. The end result truly was a new helicopter – not merely a rebuilt one – and thus the new serial numbers.

All existing CH-47 models, A, B, or C, could be put through this process. In fact, the three prototypes for the CH-47D program were originally of different model numbers. The first aircraft, 65-08008, was a CH-47A, while 67-18479 was a CH-47B, and 67-18538 represented the CH-47C.

Among the biggest improvements found in the D model were increased redundancy in the electrical and hydraulic systems. The CH-47Ds featured improved engines in the form of Lycoming T55-L-712 turbines, each of which developed 4,075 s.h.p. at takeoff. Through gearboxes these engines turned fiberglass blades with a 32-inch cord (eight inches wider than the blades on the CH-47C), providing greater lift. New, armored crew seats were added, as were AN/APR-39V radar warning and AN/ALQ-156 missile detection equipment. The fuel system was improved and made crash resistant, and armor protection was added for the transmission and oil coolers. For protection against shoulder-fired missiles, an M130 flare dispenser was added to the port side.

With the improvements, the CH-47D has a maximum gross weight of 50,000 pounds, and can transport 44 combat-ready troops. A multi-hook external cargo system allows transport of sling loads of up to 28,000 pounds at speeds up to 115 miles per hour. The triple hook system also allows the CH-47D to transport loads to multiple destinations simultaneously. The intention of the program was that the CH-47D would add about 20 years to the airframe life. As of 2014, 42 U.S. CH-47Ds had been lost in accidents, and seven lost in combat.

The initial CH-47D prototype first flew on 14 May 1979. Preparations began at Boeing's Pennsylvania facility for series production the next year, with the first production D model making its maiden flight on 26 February 1982. The initial production aircraft were delivered to the 159th Assault Helicopter Battalion, 101st Airborne Division, Fort Campbell, Kentucky, on 28 February 1983.

The CH-47D program reprocessed 441 Chinooks, including 164 CH-47A, 75 CH-47B, and 200 CH-47C aircraft. This included 11 CH-47Cs that had been built for Iran by Augusta and seven from Australia. One aircraft, serial number 84-24166, crashed during a Boeing test flight and was not delivered to the Army. Two new CH-47Ds were built from the ground up, serial numbers 92-00367, 92-00368) and a third new build, 98-02000 was put together from left-over bits and pieces at the Boeing plant, and was fittingly dubbed "Mr. Potato Head."

CH-47D airframes are under construction. Visible on the airframe in the foreground are the pitot-tube posts on the nose; the stressed-metal access doors that doubled as work platforms on the front pylon, and the channel for the main transmission driveshaft and various lines, which will receive a hinged cover along the length of the fuselage spine. The external engines and drive train made for fewer obstructions in the cargo compartment. (Army Aviation Museum)

The CH-47F, an improved version of the CH-47D, features upgraded Honeywell T55 engines rated at 4,868 s.h.p.; a revised airframe with easier inspection, maintenance, and repairs, less vibration, and longer service life; and improved avionics. The CH-47F first flew in 2001, and deliveries began in November 2006 with serial number 04-08071. Here, members of Bravo Company, 1st Battalion, 214th Aviation Regiment (General Support), conduct phase maintenance on a CH-47F at Katterbach Army Airfield, Bavaria, Germany, on 30 November 2016. (DVIDS)

As the 20th century came to a close, the Chinook was again upgraded. The latest model, the CH-47F incorporated advanced avionics. In the cockpit, the analog dials of the earlier Chinooks gave way to the Common Avionics Architecture System (CAAS) featuring five Multifunction Displays (MFD) replacing the old analog instruments. Another major avionics upgrade is the Digital Advanced Flight Control System (DAFCS) which provides unprecedented automatic hover control.

The structure of the aircraft was also improved. Larger, but fewer, components, resulted in less vibration, and inherently less maintenance. Powering the 21st-century chopper is a pair of Honeywell T55-L-714A engines, each developing 4,868 shaft horsepower.

The first three Engineering and Manufacturing Development (EMD) CH-47Fs, serial numbers 98-00011, 98-00012, and 03-08003, were remanufactured from CH-47D models, serial numbers 83-24107, 83-24115, and 83-24121. The first flight of the CH-47F model was in 2001. The rollout of the first production CH-47F took place on 15 June 2006 and the first flight was on 23 October 2006.

While about half of the CH-47Fs produced have been built new from the ground up, the balance of the production was accomplished by removing certain key components from existing CH-47D aircraft and incorporating those components into the new airframe. Given that the CH-47Ds were themselves the result of an upgrade program, the result of this is that some aircraft have had multiple lives. CH-47A 63-07906, for example, was delivered in June 1964, served in Vietnam, was converted into CH-47D 87-00096 in 1988, and deployed to Afghanistan. In 2012 it became CH-47F 13-08109.

An early-production CH-47F Chinook is under construction at the then-new Boeing Factory in Ridley Park, Pennsylvania. At the time this photograph was taken, it was expected that the factory would be delivering six CH-47Fs per month by 2013. (Army)

A CH-47F Chinook helicopter equipped with skis on the landing gear flies over a landing zone, having just dropped off paratroopers of a joint U.S. Army-Japan Ground Self-Defense Force team during Exercise Arctic Aurora in Alaska on 9 June 2016. (DVIDS)

A CH-47F from the 12th Combat Aviation Brigade is preparing to airlift by sling an M777 155mm howitzer from Archer Battery, Field Artillery Squadron, 2nd Cavalry Regiment, during an exercise at Grafenwöhr Training Area, Germany, on 21 March 2016. (DVIDS)

CH-47F serial number 13-08432 undergoes phase maintenance in a hangar of Bravo Company, 1st Battalion, 214th Aviation Regiment (General Support), at Katterbach Army Airfield, Germany, on 30 November 2016. (DVIDS)

The crew chief of Colorado Army National Guard CH-47F registration number 09-08824 checks the sound of the engines before takeoff at the Army Aviation Support Facility, Buckley Air Force Base, Colorado, on 3 March 2016. (DVIDS)

A U.S. Army CH-47F Chinook from 5th Battalion, 159th Aviation Regiment, based at Fort Eustis, Virginia, taxis at Hurlburt Field, Florida, on 7 May 2016 during Exercise Emerald Warrior 16, a U.S. Special Operations Command readiness exercise. (DVIDS)

The MH-47 series was designed for use in special forces operations and features a long refueling probe for inflight fuel replenishment, a fast-rope rappelling system, and further improvements. Of the 12 MH-47Ds delivered starting in 1983, half were converted from CH-47As and the remainder from CH-47Cs. Also delivered starting in 1991 were the MH-47Es (conversions from CH-47Cs), which had provisions for more fuel as well as terrain-following/avoidance radar. More recently, deliveries of the MH-47G began in 2004. The MH-47s were assigned to the 160th Special Operations Aviation Regiment (Airborne) "Nightstalkers," based at Fort Campbell Kentucky. Here, an MH-47 hovers while special forces troops leap off the ramp into the water.

Aircraft of the MH-47 family are specifically equipped for use by Special Operations Heavy Assault Helicopter Companies. These Chinooks are among the variety of specialized helicopters operated by the 160th Special Operations Aviation Regiment (Airborne) – SOAR(A), based at Fort Campbell, Kentucky.

Three models of the MH-47 have been fielded since the first of the type, the MH-47D, was introduced in the mid-1980s. The 12 MH-47Ds were converted from existing aircraft through the addition of nose radar, an infrared camera, satellite communications, electronic countermeasures, improved navigational systems, and most externally visible, an inflight refueling probe and all-black paint job.

The 26 MH-47E models, introduced in 1991, incorporated all the features of the MH-47D, but added terrain-following radar, improved avionics, Lycoming T55-L-714 engines, an external rescue hoist, and most noticeably, enlarged fuel tanks, which doubled the integral fuel capacity.

The latest model of Special Operations Chinook is the MH-47G, which combines the new CH-47F airframe with the attributes of the MH-47E, including enlarged fuel tanks. Additionally, the MH-47G includes a special-operations Common Avionics Architecture System (CAAS) avionics package as well as multi-mode radar with terrain following/ terrain avoidance and weather detection. The MH-47G is equipped for use with Fast Rope Insertion and Extraction (FRIES) and the Special Patrol Insertion & Extraction System (SPIES). Armament of the MH-47G is formidable, with two M134 Miniguns as well as two M240D machine guns.

During an infiltration training exercise, members of the U.S. Air Force's 23rd Special Tactics Squadron fitted out as frogmen jump off the lowered ramp of an MH-47 Chinook Helicopter at Wynnehaven Beach, Florida, on 9 April 2013.

During a training exercise off South Korea, an MH-47 from the 160th Special Operations Aviation Regiment (Airborne) is taking on fuel from an MC-130P Combat Shadow in March 2009. At the time, the 160th SOAR was deployed from Fort Lewis, Washington.

An MH-47 Chinook of the 160th Special Operations Aviation Regiment (Airborne) lifts off from the flight deck of USS Wasp (LHD-1) during the ship's deck-landing qualification. Markings were conspicuously absent from these special-ops helicopters.

Before making their name in the Vietnam War, Chinook helicopters operated Stateside in the early 1960s. Cruising in view of the Empire State Building in Midtown Manhattan, this CH-47A, serial number 64-13122, was delivered to the U.S. Army on 10 March 1965.

Two U.S. Army CH-47A medium helicopters fly in formation during a training exercise at Fort Rucker on 4 February 1963. The closer Chinook was serial number 60-3450, the third production CH-47, which was delivered on 29 June 1962. (National Archives)

This rear view of the fourth production CH-47A Chinook, serial number 60-3450, illustrates a key identifying feature of the -A model: the sharp rear vertical edge of the aft rotor pylon. Near the base of the pylon is the exhaust for the auxiliary power unit.

The U.S. Army shipped CH-47A Chinook helicopters to the Republic of Vietnam in large numbers beginning with the shipment of 1st Cavalry Division (Air Mobile) Chinooks seen here, arriving aboard the carrier USS Boxer at Quy Nhơn, Republic of Vietnam, on 13 September 1965. (National Archives)

Boeing Vertol CH-47A Chinooks, interspersed with Bell UH-1 helicopters, are lined up on the flight deck of USS Boxer upon arrival at Quy Nhơn, South Vietnam, on 13 September 1965. For the voyage, sealants and protective covers had been applied to the helicopters and the rotors removed. (National Archives)

CH-47A 64-13127 of 1st Cavalry Division (Air Mobile) is being spotted on the flight deck of USS *Boxer*. The helicopters were stripped of protective materials, the rotors were installed, systems were checked, and the Chinooks flew off from the deck for land. (National Archives)

To take part in Operation Abilene, a search-and-destroy mission, a CH-47A airlifts members of Company C, 2nd Battalion, 18th Infantry, to a site near Xã Cẩm Mỹ, southeast of Saigon, South Vietnam, on 2 April 1966. Chinooks in Vietnam were painted matte Olive Drab. (National Archives)

Chinooks quickly proved their worth as troop and cargo transporters in Vietnam. Here, a CH-47A delivers supplies to Battery C, 2nd Battalion, 7th Artillery, during Operation Crazy Horse, a search-and-destroy mission in the Vĩnh Thạnh Valley on 25 May 1966. (National Archives)

A CH-47A helicopter carries artillery ammunition in slings in order to resupply Battery C, 2nd Battalion, 19th Artillery, in the Vĩnh Thạnh Valley in Bình Định Province on 25 May 1966. CH-47As soon proved to be underpowered for operations in the extreme heat of Vietnam. (National Archives)

Occasionally, a Chinook was the subject of an airlift instead of the instigator, as in this case of a Sikorsky CH-54 Tarhe helicopter transporting a CH-54A that had crashed in An Khê. The fuselage of the Chinook seems mostly intact, but both rotor pylons are missing. (National Archives)

On 26 August 1966, a CH-47A is about to take on a slingload of 105mm howitzer ammunition at Ammunition Supply Point (ASP) Oasis for transport to an artillery unit in the field. A soldier on the ground is holding a sling, ready to attach it to the cargo hook. (National Archives)

In May 1966, three of the four ACH-47 gunships arrived in Vietnam with the 53rd Aviation Detachment, for evaluation in combat. Here, a trooper is loading ammunition for the 40mm grenade launcher. The insignia of the 53rd AD is on the front rotor pylon. (Army Aviation Museum)

A member of the 53rd Aviation Detachment checks the armor plates attached to the forward part of the fuselage of an ACH-47, to provide protection to the flight crew from small-arms fire. To the left is the 40mm flex feed chute with its cover removed. (Army Aviation Museum)

Seen in Vietnam is the left-hand installation of an XM159 19-round 2.75-inch rocket-launcher pod and an M24A1 20mm cannon on a Boeing Vertol ACH-47A. A full complement of 19 of the 2.75-inch rockets are loaded into the launcher pod. (Army Aviation Museum)

A member of the 53rd Aviation Detachment makes adjustments to the feed mechanism of an M24A1 20mm cannon mounted on the right stub wing of an ACH-47A helicopter. These gunships were nicknamed "Guns A-Go-Go" and "Go-Go Birds." (Army Aviation Museum)

Two soldiers load 2.75-inch rockets into the right launcher pod of an ACH-47A, while two others look into a hatch on the right fuselage sponson, inside which is the transformer/rectifier cooling fan. To the right is a window-mounted .50-caliber machine gun. (National Archives)

Specialist 4th Class John Gunther, a .50-caliber gunner, loads a machine gun on the left side of an ACH-47A Chinook on 21 September 1966. Chromate green primer is on the upper part of the cargo compartment, while a gray paint is on the lower half. (National Archives)

A member of the 53rd Aviation Detachment (Field Evaluation) (Provisional) lugs an XM159 19-round 2.75-inch rocket-launcher pod on his shoulder while walking by an ACH-47A gun ship that has a partially loaded 19-round rocket pod on its left stub wing. (National Archives)

"Easy Money" is the nickname painted in white on the fuselage aft of the cockpit of this ACH-47A being readied for a combat mission on 21 September 1966. The three ACH-47s were supporting the 1st Cavalry Division, lending fire support for ground troops. (National Archives)

An ACH-47A from the 53rd Aviation Detachment (Field Evaluation) (Provisional) is visible through the open window of another ACH-47A of the same unit during a combat mission on 21 September 1966. This unit evaluated ACH-47s from June to October 1966. (National Archives)

A .50-caliber machine gunner in an ACH-47A observes the ground below for enemy targets. Below the machine gun is a metal bin for channeling spent casings to the collection bag below it. To the right of the gun is its feed chute and ammunition box. (Army Aviation Museum)

These CH-47As of the 228th Aviation Battalion (Assault Support Helicopter), 1st Cavalry Division (Airmobile) are engaged in a resupply mission in support of Operation Thayer on 28 September 1966. On the ground are 500-gallon portable fuel tanks. (National Archives)

On 28 September 1966, the CH-47A helicopter pad at An Khê, Republic of Vietnam, is viewed facing to the south. These Chinooks of 228th Aviation Battalion (Assault Support Helicopter) were being prepared to resupply ground troops in Operation Thayer. (National Archives)

A ¼-ton truck disembarks from CH-47A serial number 66-0069 from 228th Aviation Battalion in support of Operation Thayer, a 1st Cavalry Division (Airborne) search-and-destroy mission conducted 45 kilometers northeast of An Khê, on 28 September 1966. (National Archives)

CH-47 serial number 61-3144 from Company B, 228th Aviation Battalion, is framed in the round window of another Chinook on 28 September 1966. Both helicopters were standing by prior to commencing a resupply mission for troops taking part in Operation Thayer. (National Archives)

During Operation Irving, a 1st Cavalry Division search-and-destroy operation against the Việt Cộng in Phù Mỹ District, Bình Định Province, on 10 and 11 October 1966, CH-47A serial number 64-13124 is picking up members of the 8th Cavalry Regiment for airlift into combat. (National Archives)

Troops of the 1st Engineer Battalion, 1st Cavalry Division, rappel from a CH-47A during Operation Cedar Falls, a massive search-and-destroy mission in the Iron Triangle just north of Saigon in Bình Dương Province, in January 1967. They would use chainsaws and explosives to clear a landing zone. (National Archives)

CH-47As, with their capacity to carry many stretcher or ambulatory patients, often served as medevac helicopters. This Chinook has just brought a wounded soldier to a base, where the awaiting Dodge M43 ambulance will take him to a field hospital, on 6 June 1967. (National Archives)

Chinooks in Vietnam assisted artillery units to move their pieces into firing positions and then quickly move them to new positions. Here, a Chinook of the 213th Aviation Company is airlifting a 105mm howitzer during Operation Billings on 10 June 1967. (National Archives)

On 6 July 1967, a CH-47 is preparing to airlift supplies back to the base at Củ Chi during Operation Kole Kole, a 25th Infantry Division search-and-destroy mission. To the left, a soldier is standing on a pack of supplies, ready to attach the sling to the cargo hook. (National Archives)

A CH-47A, serial number 65-8023, is airlifting a 105mm howitzer to a base camp at Tân Uyên, near Long Bình, in mid-August 1967. On the aft rotor pylon is a white, red, and white flash. The upper part of the ramp is retracted into the lower half of the ramp. (National Archives)

On 21 or 22 August 1967, a CH-47 Chinook lifts supplies for the construction of a forward base camp at the intersections of two canals in Quảng Nam Province during Operation Shelbyville, sometimes referred to as "Operation Shelby." On the aft rotor pylon is a white, pentagonal insignia with a diagonal red stripe across it. (National Archives)

In a companion view to the preceding photo, taken on 21 or 22 August 1967 during Operation Shelby, a CH-47 is bringing in a slingload of sandbags for the construction of defenses at a forward base in Quảng Nam Province. There is a white "X" is on the aft rotor pylon. (National Archives)

Members of an ARVN unit prepare to fasten a slung 155mm howitzer to a hovering CH-47 in January 1969. The presence of a strake on the fuselage sponson identifies this Chinook as a CH-47B or CH-47C. A gunner next to an M60 machine gun looks out the door. (National Archives)

The U.S. Army and Boeing/Vertol conducted single-engine-landing tests with this CH-47 at Lake Tahoe Airport in Nevada on 27 January 1969. The tests were to determine the CH-47's height-velocity curve, which set the parameters for safe and unsafe flight profiles. (National Archives)

A CH-47 that was damaged by rocket shrapnel during a Việt Cộng attack on Tân Sơn Nhứt Airbase is observed at close range in a hangar in May 1968. The access door on the nose is propped open. The dark red upholstery of the two seats in the cockpit is in view. (Bob Steinbrunn)

The Chinook helicopter to the right is being refueled at the base of the 228th Supply and Service Company, 277th Supply and Service Battalion, Tây Ninh Province, Republic of Vietnam, while another Chinook is preparing to land, on 19 April 1970. (National Archives)

A CH-47 Chinook stirs up considerable dust as it is about to touch down at Landing Zone Bronco during the incursion into Cambodia in late June 1970. The helicopter was on a medevac mission to extract wounded troops for treatment at a rear-area hospital. (National Archives)

Soldiers secure a sling of materiel to the cargo hook of a CH-47A at Landing Zone Bronco in Cambodia, for return to Vietnam on 23 or 24 June 1970. Cargo handlers found that the area directly under the low-hovering Chinook was surprisingly calm. (National Archives)

The 1st Cavalry Division (Airborne) crest is on the aft rotor pylon of this CH-47A from which troops are disembarking at Landing Zone Ramada in Cambodia on 23 or 24 June 1970. They are pushing what appears to be a mechanical mule down the ramp. (National Archives)

Troopers from the 8th Cavalry Regiment, 1st Cavalry Division, board a CH-47A, serial number 66-0074, at Fire Support Base Condor for transport back to Vietnam during the Cambodian Incursion, on 27 June 1970. A white-blue-white flash is on the aft pylon. (National Archives)

A Chinook is about to lift a slingload of crates and cargo at Fire Base David, operated by the 1st Brigade, 1st Cavalry Division (Airmobile) near Ou Reang in Cambodia in mid-July 1970. The absence of strakes on the rears of the sponsons marks this as a CH-47A. (National Archives)

A soldier secures the "doughnut ring" of a sling to the cargo hook of a Chinook medium helicopter hovering just feet off the ground. The sling contains packing tubes for heavy artillery ammunition; unpacked projectiles lie on the ground to the left. (National Archives)

Two slings full of cargo are fastened to the cargo hook of a CH-47A Chinook, lifting off from Fire Base David, Ou Reang, Cambodia in mid-July 1970. Slung loads accounted for much, if not most, of the cargo the Chinooks airlifted in the Indochina war. (National Archives)

Fitted with ski landing gear, a CH-47 Chinook is about to land on Trident Glacier, south of Fort Greely, Alaska, during a training exercise for operating on glaciers conducted by the Northern Warfare Training Center, Fort Greely, in September 1970. (National Archives)

CH-47A serial number 65-7990 is being prepared to transport supplies from the helipad of Company C, 3rd Signal Battalion, 45 miles out of Saigon, to troops atop Hill 837, Núi Chứa Chan. Chinooks could resupply the most isolated outposts. (National Archives)

A soldier of the 175th Aviation Company refuels a CH-47 at the base at Cần Thơ in the Mekong Delta of South Vietnam, in 1970. The tanker truck has parked as close as possible to the Chinook. The helicopter's fueling port was below an access hatch in the forward end of the right sponson. This was a single-point fueling station, permitting the filling of all of the fuel tanks from one filler. (National Archives)

Window-mounted M60D 7.62mm machine guns in CH-47 helicopters gave the aircrews the means of laying down suppressive fire when approaching or departing from contested landing zones. The M60D was designed for flexible mounts in vehicles and aircraft, and was equipped with two spade grips (bottom left of photo) rather than the M60's pistol grip. A fold-down ring sight was installed on the receiver. (National Archives)

A crew chief from the 147th Aviation Company is ready to guide a CH-47 Chinook out of a revetment in preparation for a mission at Cần Thơ, Republic of Vietnam, during 1970. Cần Thơ was a major airbase in the Mekong Delta. (National Archives)

A member of Battery B, 3rd Battalion, 82nd Artillery Regiment, watches a CH-47A descend for a landing at Fire Base Center, Tây Ninh, South Vietnam, in 1970. The dark spot on the Chinook's belly marks the location of the cargo hook. (National Archives)

In Vietnam, the Chinook seemingly had a thousand uses. Here, a CH-47 from the 213th Assault Helicopter Company, 145th Aviation Battalion, hovers over a pond, collecting large buckets of water to dump on a grass fire on 5 July 1971. (National Archives)

A helicopter from the 213th Assault Helicopter Company, 145th Aviation Battalion, dumps water onto a grass fire in South Vietnam on 5 July 1971. A red and white roundel is on the aft pylon. (National Archives)

Troops load their baggage in a Chinook during an evacuation of civilians and nonessential U.S. military personnel at Kon Tum, Republic of Vietnam, on 3 May 1972. The tail number 8541 likely indicates that this was CH-47C serial number 67-18541. (National Archives)

Troops unload supplies from a CH-47 at a base camp during training maneuvers on the Eklatuna ice field, Fort Richardson, Alaska, in January 1973. High-visibility orange paint on the Chinook's front and rear is an aid for potential rescuers. (National Archives)

A CH-47B or -C from the 213th Aviation Company (Assault Support Helicopter) based at Camp Humphreys, Republic of Korea, is positioned to lift a TRAC 120 communications van from the Highpoint Signal Site, near Pyeongtaek, on 7 June 1973. (National Archives)

An emergency repair shelter covers the aft part of a CH-47 at Fort Wainwright, Alaska, on 24 April 1974. The U.S. Army Arctic Test Center was conducting evaluations on this new shelter. An external heater unit is pumping warm air into the shelter. (National Archives)

Army paratroopers in winter camouflage parkas prepare for a static-line jump from a CH-47 Chinook during Exercise Jack Frost '75 out of Eielson Air Force Base, Alaska, in January 1975. Quilted soundproofing insulation lines the compartment. (National Archives)

During an annual service practice at an Eighth Army range near Daecheon Beach, Republic of Korea, in the spring of 1976, a CH-47 Chinook uses a sling to lift a 1,500-pound Ryan Firebee target drone back to its helipad. (National Archives)

A CH-47C lands a Chaparral antiaircraft missile launcher during a field exercise near Kaiserslautern, West Germany, in about October 1976 – the first time the launchers had been airlifted to a launch site under operational conditions. (National Archives)

During a training exercise at Fort Bragg, North Carolina, on 1 December 1977, a CH-47C of the 196th Aviation Company has just dropped a container from the cargo compartment. The static line that will actuate the container's parachute is faintly visible. (National Archives)

A CH-47 Chinook helicopter serving with the 6th Cavalry lowers a section of a pontoon bridge into the Cowhouse River during the joint-services Operation Gallant Crew '77. Using a medium-lift helicopter in this manner made for relatively quick bridge-building.

On 17 July 1978, a CH-47 lifts a stripped 6x6 truck as part of a test of the effect of the slung load on an AN/ASN-128 Lightweight Doppler Navigation System installed in the Chinook. This helicopter also was equipped with a prototype multi-hook system. (National Archives)

A CH-47B or -C airlifts a UH-1 medevac helicopter that has crashed during a rescue mission in the Colorado Rockies on 15 August 1978. The number 505 is painted in white on the flattened trailing edge of the Chinook's aft rotor pylon. Cords secure the UH-1's rotors to keep them from whipping around. In Vietnam and after the war, Chinooks chalked up an impressive record of recovering downed aircraft. (National Archives)

Army mechanics service the engine and rotor of a CH-47. The engine access panels are hinged forward. Above the engine, a stressed-metal access hatch serves as a work platform for the kneeling mechanic. Access doors on the front of the pylon are open.

A mechanic makes adjustments to the left engine's quick-disconnect shelf: a fitting attached to the bottom of the engine that contains quick-release couplings for engine wiring, fuel, and hydraulic components, enabling rapid change-outs of the engine.

During Exercise Sentry Castle '81 at Fort Drum, New York, in July 1981, an Army CH-47A, as indicated by the lack of strakes and the sharp leading edge of the aft pylon, is in a hover as an Aggressor Forces M48A5 main battle tank advances through a field.

A CH-47C Chinook helicopter (with a pitot tube on the nose), numbered 526 on the forward rotor pylon, has landed with supplies at the base encampment area of the Korean Tactical Range in February 1982. A black-cat insignia is on the aft rotor pylon.

The same CH-47C seen in the preceding photo is in a low-level hover during a resupply mission to the base encampment area of the Korean Tactical Range in February 1982. This Chinook had several Tan-colored skin panels in addition to the overall Olive Drab.

Three CH-47 Chinook helicopters fly in formation over an airbase during Exercise Ocean Venture '82, a joint air, sea, and ground readiness exercise in the Caribbean in April and May 1982. Flare dispensers are visible, jutting from the rears of the fuselages.

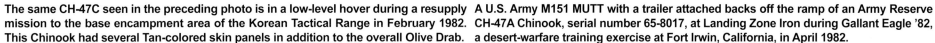

A U.S. Army M151 MUTT with a trailer attached backs off the ramp of an Army Reserve CH-47A Chinook, serial number 65-8017, at Landing Zone Iron during Gallant Eagle '82, a desert-warfare training exercise at Fort Irwin, California, in April 1982.

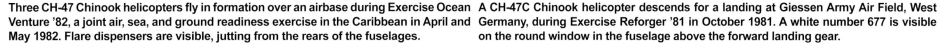

A CH-47C Chinook helicopter descends for a landing at Giessen Army Air Field, West Germany, during Exercise Reforger '81 in October 1981. A white number 677 is visible on the round window in the fuselage above the forward landing gear.

Members of Battery A, 2nd Battalion, 31st Field Artillery, hook a sling from an M198 155mm howitzer to cargo hooks on a CH-47B or -C during Exercise Eagle Strike III at Fort Campbell, Kentucky, in December 1982. The M198 howitzer weighs 15,772 pounds.

A CH-47C Chinook helicopter flies at low level during a tactical retrograde exercise for Operation Bear Hunt '84. This was a readiness exercise held in the Republic of Korea in October 1964. Tail number 22276 is faintly visible, likely indicating serial 74-22276.

Members of a mortar team from the 1st Battalion, 21st Infantry, 25th Infantry Division, prepare to board a CH-47 Chinook helicopter for a practice air assault during the joint South Korean/U.S. training exercise, Team Spirit '84, in March 1984.

A CH-47C is about to lift an M102 105mm howitzer off the ground during the joint U.S./Honduran field-training Exercise Ahuas Tara II (Big Pine) in May 1984. Near the top of the aft rotor pylon is a blue silhouette of a porpoise, with "FLIPPER" written above it.

Red crew seats are visible through the windows of this CH-47C Chinook at Sainte-Mère-Église on or around 6 June 1984. The helicopter was participating in a ceremony to commemorate the 40th anniversary of D-Day, the Allied invasion of Europe.

NASA, in cooperation with the U.S. Army, operated a CH-47B to test improved flight-control systems at Ames Research Center during 1985. The tail number 737 was applied to this helicopter, which was painted overall in white, with dark-blue trim. (NASA)

Men of the 320th General Support Aviation Company perform maintenance on a CH-47 during disaster relief in Colombia after the eruption of a volcano. Two of the men stand on a built-in work platform. The hinged spine containing the drive shaft is open.

Transporting personnel and supplies, a U.S. Army CH-47D Chinook takes off from the helipad of the battleship USS *Iowa* (BB-61) in January 1987. The ship was visiting Puerto Cortés, Honduras, for a civic-action program.

Three CH-47 Chinook helicopters airlift artillery pieces in support of air-assault units during a joint U.S. Air Force and U.S. Army air-drop/air-assault exercise at the Darlington County Airport, South Carolina, in October 1987.

The same three CH-47 Chinook helicopters shown in the preceding photo are seen from a different angle during an airlift of artillery pieces at the Darlington County Airport. Chinooks were instrumental in giving artillery batteries the ability to "shoot and scoot."

A CH-47 Chinook helicopter descends for a landing onto a temporary helipad at the 129th Evacuation Hospital field station during the mass-casualty phase of the joint U.S./South Korean Exercise Team Spirit '87 at Osan, Republic of Korea, during 1987.

Medics from the 129th Evacuation Hospital carry wounded soldiers on stretchers from the rear of a CH-47 during the mass-casualty phase of Team Spirit '87. The CH-47 could carry 24 stretcher patients in three tiers per side, four stretchers high per tier.

Members of the 129th Evacuation Hospital prepare to remove simulated stretcher patients from a CH-47 during Team Spirit '87. Rigid brackets support the outboard sides of the stretcher rails, while the inboard sides are held by straps and clamps.

A CH-47D Chinook helicopter takes off from a clearing at Palmerola Air Base, Honduras, during the joint Honduran/U.S. Exercise Cabanas '88. A characteristic of the CH-47D, three cargo hooks on the belly are visible here in silhouette.

As part of a foreign-assistance road-construction project by members of the West Virginia Army National Guard in Honduras in March 1983, a CH-47D Chinook serves as a flying crane, airlifting sections of a concrete culvert to the point where they are needed.

57

A CH-47D, recognizable by the large opening in the front of the aft pylon, uses slings to airlift four potable-water bladders to the field during Operation Golden Pheasant in Honduras in March 1988. The bladders are marked "DRINKING WATER ONLY."

Equipped with skis on the landing gear for possible operations on snow, a CH-47C Chinook is airlifting 105mm howitzers of Battery A, 4th Battalion, 11th Field Artillery, to Drop Zone Husky during combined Army-Air Force live-fire exercises Calfex IV at the Yukon Command Training Site, Eielson Air Force Base, Alaska, in September 1988.

A CH-47 lowers a 105mm howitzer assigned to Battery A, 4th Battalion, 11th Field Artillery, onto Drop Zone Husky during Calfex IV, combined Army-Air Force live-fire Exercises at the Yukon Command Training Site, Eielson Air Force Base, Alaska.

In the foreground, a member of a ground-support crew, wearing an orange and yellow high-visibility vest and a Kevlar helmet, signals to the pilot of a CH-47 Chinook who is approaching to attempt to retrieve the container in the background. This operation transpired during Exercise Team Spirit '89 in the Republic of Korea.

In a continuation of the operation depicted in the preceding view, the member of the ground support crew has arms stretched out to signal the pilot of a CH-47 Chinook helicopter while he maneuvers close to the ground, to enable the two handlers under the helicopter to secure a container to the 'copter's cargo hook.

A ground crewman hauls a fuel hose up to a CH-47 Chinook in preparation for refueling the helicopter at Bradshaw Air Field, Pohakuloa Training Area, Hawaii, during the 21st Infantry Division's annual field exercises during 1988.

Members of 1st Battalion, 325th Airborne Infantry Regiment, use slings to secure an M102 105mm towed howitzer and an M998 HMMWV to a CH-47D after a firing demonstration for Saudi Arabian national guardsmen during Operation Desert Shield.

Two U.S. Army CH-47 Chinook helicopters, including in the foreground a CH-47D with the number 57 in a window, are lifting slung M102 105mm light towed howitzers during the joint-service exercise Ocean Venture '90 in Puerto Rico in January 1990.

In an image probably captured just taken minutes after the preceding view, a CH-47D airlifts an M998 HMMWV with an M102 105mm howitzer hitched to it. The vehicle and howitzer were from the 1st Battalion, 325th Airborne Infantry Regiment.

Through a haze of dust, U.S. Army CH-47 Chinook helicopters take off from a site in Saudi Arabia on a mission during Operation Desert Shield, the buildup phase that lasted from 2 August 1990 to 17 January 1991, prior to the expulsion of Iraqi forces from Kuwait.

Two soldiers of the 82nd Airborne Division observe a Chinook preparing to touch down at a site in Saudi Arabia during Operation Desert Shield. This is a CH-47D, as indicated by the three cargo hooks and the opening in the front of the aft rotor pylon.

A line of CH-47 Chinooks (left) and UH-60 Blackhawk helicopters (right) assembled at Jacksonville, Florida, are clad in protective covers, except for the landing gear, for shipment to the Middle East in support of Operation Desert Shield in August 1990.

Kurdish refugees have a look at a U.S. Army CH-47D that will transport them to a new refugee camp in northern Iraq in April 1991. Above the two pitot tubes on the nose are radar-warning antennas. Below the nose ar e retractable, aimable taxiing lights.

The same window gunner featured in the preceding photo is seen at another moment, manning a .50-caliber M2 machine gun. This mount is in the forward left window of the cargo compartment; to the far right, the passageway to the cockpit is visible.

Soldiers from A Company, 4th Battalion 87th Infantry, 25th Infantry Division, are boarding a CH-47 on 3 March 1995 after conducting a company-size patrol of Le Borgne, Haiti, and vicinity in a peacekeeping operation code named Uphold Democracy.

In May 1991 a gunner in a U.S. Army CH-47 Chinook stands by next to a window-mounted .50-caliber machine gun during operations in support of Operation Provide Comfort, efforts to aid Kurdish refugees who fled the forces of Saddam Hussein in northern Iraq in the wake of Operation Desert Storm. He is leaning on the ammunition box for the gun, containing 100 rounds of linked .50-caliber ammo.

Specifications

	CH-47A	CH-47B	CH-47C	CH-47D	CH-47F	MH-47D	MH-47E	MH-47G
DIMENSIONS	feet, inches							
Length, Rotors	98 ft., 1.3 in.	98 ft., 11 in.	98 ft., 11 in.	98 ft., 11 in.	98 ft., 11 in.	98 ft., 11 in.	98 ft., 11 in.	98 ft., 11 in.
Length, Fuselage	50 ft., 9 in.	50 ft., 9 in.	50 ft., 9 in.	50 ft., 9 in.	50 ft., 9 in.	52 ft., 1 in.	52 ft., 1 in.	52 ft., 1 in.
Width over Fuel	12 ft., 5 in.	12 ft., 5 in.	12 ft., 5 in.	12 ft., 5 in.	12 ft., 5 in.	12 ft., 5 in.	12 ft., 5 in.	12 ft., 5 in.
Height (top of aft rotor head)	18 ft., 6 in.	18 ft., 6 in.	18 ft., 6 in.	18 ft., 6 in.	18 ft., 6 in.	18 ft., 6 in.	18 ft., 6 in.	18 ft., 6 in.
Rotor Diameter	59 ft., 1.25 in.	60 ft., 0 in.	60 ft., 0 in.	60 ft., 0 in.	60 ft., 0 in.	60 ft., 0 in.	60 ft., 0 in.	60 ft., 0 in.
Wheelbase	22 ft., 10 in.	22 ft., 10 in.	22 ft., 10 in.	22 ft., 10 in.	22 ft., 10 in.	22 ft., 10 in.	22 ft., 10 in.	22 ft., 10 in.
Cabin Length	30 ft., 6 in.	30 ft., 6 in.	30 ft., 6 in.	30 ft., 6 in.	30 ft., 6 in.	30 ft., 6 in.	30 ft., 6 in.	30 ft., 6 in.
Cabin Width	7 ft., 6 in.	7 ft., 6 in.	7 ft., 6 in.	7 ft., 6 in.	7 ft., 6 in.	7 ft., 6 in.	7 ft., 6 in.	7 ft., 6 in.
Cabin Height	6 ft., 6 in. / 2.0	6 ft., 6 in. / 2.0	6 ft., 6 in. / 2.0	6 ft., 6 in. / 2.0	6 ft., 6 in. / 2.0	6 ft., 6 in. / 2.0	6 ft., 6 in. / 2.0	6 ft., 6 in. / 2.0
FUEL	gallons							
Integral	621	621*	1,100**	1,034	1,034	10,34	2,068	2,068
Auxiliary (Maximum)	none	none	none	2,400	2,400	2,400	2,400	2,400
In-Flight Refueling	No	No	No	No	No	Yes	Yes	Yes
WEIGHTS	pounds							
Empty Weight	18,288 lbs	19,676 lbs	21,586 lbs	23,729 lbs	24,000	23,729 lbs	26,918 lbs	26,918 lbs
Maximum Gross Weight	33,000 lbs	40,000 lbs	46,000 lbs	50,000 lbs	50,000 lbs	50,000 lbs	54,000 lbs	54,000 lbs
PERFORMANCE								
Maximum Cruising Speed	110 knots	155 knots	161 knots	158 knots	158 knots	158 knots	140 knots	160 knots
Maximum Speed	130 knots	165 knots		163 knots	170 knots	170 knots	154 knots	170 knots
Cruising Speed (SL)	110 knots	140 knots	150 knots	130 knots	130 knots	130 knots	140 knots	130 knots
Service Ceiling	11,900 feet	16,300 feet	15,000 feet	20,000 feet	20,000 feet	20,000 feet	20,000 feet	20,000 feet
Single Hook Capacity	16,000 pounds	20,000 pounds	20,000 pounds	26,000 pounds	26,000 pounds	26,000 pounds	26,000 pounds	26,000 pounds
Forward or Aft Hook	not applicable	not applicable	not applicable	17,000 pounds	17,000 pounds	17,000 pounds	17,000 pounds	17,000 pounds
ENGINES	shaft horsepower							
Type	T55-L-7C	T55-L-7C	T55-L-11	T55-L-712A	T55-L-714A	T55-L-712A	T55-L-714A	T55-L-714A
Maximum Power	2,850	2,850	3,750	3,750	4,867	3,750	4,867	4,867
Normal	2,400	2,400	3,300	3,000	4,168	3,000	4,168	4,168
Military Power (30 minutes)	2,650	2,650	3,750	3,400	4,527	3,400	4,527	4,527
Emergency	–	–	–	4,500	5,069	4,500	5,069	5,069
Rotor R.P.M.	230	225/230	235/245	225	225	225	225	225

*CH-47B aircraft with crash-resistant fuel tanks had a 566-gallon / 2,143-liter total capacity.
**CH-47C aircraft with crash-resistant fuel tanks had a 1,036-gallon / 3,922-liter total capacity.

Members of the 24th Forward Support Battalion, 24th Infantry Division (Mechanized) secure a sling attached to an HMMWV to a CH-47 Chinook during sling-load training at the Remagen Drop Zone, Fort Stewart, Georgia, in January 1996.

Army and Air Force personnel maneuver a pylon and rotor assembly from an Army National Guard CH-47D Chinook down the ramp of a C-5B Galaxy at the airport at Timehri, Guyana, during New Horizon '97, a joint U.S.-Guyana humanitarian exercise.

At Kumaka, Guyana, in July 1997, two structural engineers from the 820th Red Horse Squadron, Nellis Air Force Base, Nevada, prepare to attach two sling rings onto a CH-47D Chinook in order to airlift a tractor secured to a flatbed trailer. The destination of the Chinook and its load was Camp Stephenson, Timehri, Guyana.

During the joint U.S.-Guyanese humanitarian and civic-assistance exercise depicted in the preceding image, a soldier prepares to attach a sling harness of supplies to an Iowa Army National Guard CH-47 Chinook for airlift to a remote site in Guyana.

During a training exercise at Fort Campbell, Kentucky, in 1997, an Army CH-47D Chinook lifts an HMMWV at a field-training site. The two slings from the HMMWV are attached to the forward and the aft cargo hooks on the belly of the helicopter.

A view through the center cargo hatch in the belly of a CH-47 attached to the 49th Armored Division, National Guard, shows, in the foreground, the radius bar from which the hook is suspended, below which is an HMMWV being transported by slings.

During a June 2000 field exercise, featuring simulated wounded troops at Fort Hood, Texas, medics from the 21st Combat Support Hospital await the signal to load their "casualties" into the CH-47D Chinook helicopter in the background.

The two members of the 21st Combat Support Hospital seen in the preceding photo are jumping clear of the HMMWV now that they have completed the attachment of the sling to the CH-47D and the helicopter is about to ascend at Fort Hood, Texas, in June 2000.

In a sequence similar to the two previous images, a U.S. Army CH-47 Chinook prepares to lift off, sling carrying a High-Mobility Multipurpose Wheeled Vehicle (HMMWV) and trailer, while testing new slings and transport systems at Fort Campbell, Kentucky.

During a sling-load practice exercise at Fort Hood, Texas, in June 2000, soldiers from the 21st Combat Support Hospital, 1st Medical Brigade, attach a sling from a High-Mobility Multipurpose Wheeled Vehicle (HMMWV) to the center-bay hoist of a hovering CH-47D Chinook from the 49th Armored Division, National Guard.

Two U.S. Army CH-47 Chinooks are parked on a hardstand at V.C. Bird International Airport, Antigua during the Tradewinds '02 Field Training Exercise on 11 April 2002. The numbers 69 (foreground) and 00 are marked on the trailing edges of the pylons.

A row of U.S. Army CH-47 helicopters is parked on a ramp at V.C. Bird International Airport in April 2002. On their sides, and particularly noticeable to the far right, are blister windows, for better visibility; these began to be installed on Chinooks by 1984.

This Chinook from Company G, 140th Aviation, Nevada Army National Guard, seen at V.C. Bird International Airport during Tradewinds '02, was CH-47D serial number 92-00287, which had been converted to a -D from CH-47A serial number 62-02131.

Soldiers of Bravo Company, 2nd Battalion, 20th Special Forces Group (Airborne), begin to disembark from a Chinook upon landing at Robert Bradshaw International Airport, St. Kitts Island, during the Tradewinds '02 Field Training Exercise, April 2002.

During a 3 May 2003 training mission, troopers from Troop B, 9th Cavalry, 3rd Brigade Combat Team, 4th Infantry Division, are about to jump from the rear of a Chinook, tail number 0-24355, hovering over Townsend Reservoir at Fort Carson, Colorado.

In a continuation of the action depicted in the preceding photograph, members of Troop B, 9th Cavalry, have jumped from the CH-47 helicopter into the undoubtedly chilly water of Townsend Reservoir. Such water-insertion training was essential for light-cavalry units.

With 326 marked in white on one of its round windows, a U.S. Army CH-47 has returned civilians to their village, Deh Rawood, in Urûzgân Province, Afghanistan. The villagers had been treated for wounds received in an accidental bombing during Operation Enduring Freedom on 2 August 2002.

A U.S. Army Chinook approaches to evacuate a team of soldiers from the 3rd Battalion, 505th Infantry, from the village of Gangikhel, Afghanistan, after they completed missions to seek enemy forces' weapon caches during Operation Enduring Freedom.

A U.S. Army MH-47 Chinook operated by Company B, 2nd Battalion, 160th Special Operations Aviation Regiment, based at Fort Campbell, Kentucky, is employing its winch to pull a downed aircrew member from the 128th Air Refueling Wing from Lake Michigan during part of Exercise Whitetail 2001, a water-rescue exercise conducted on Lake Michigan and in Wisconsin in August 2001.

Troops from 1st Caribbean Battalion, a composite force drawn from 14 Caribbean countries, scramble to board a CH-47 from Detachment 1, G Company, 140th Aviation, Nevada Army National Guard, in Barbuda during Exercise Tradewinds 2002. (Department of Defense)

During Operation Lifeline, a supply effort for victims of an earthquake that hit Pakistan in October 2005, a flag-emblazoned U.S. Army CH-47 hauls two sling loads of provisions for people stranded in Muẓaffarâbâd, Kashmîr Province. (Department of Defense)

U.S. Army 1st Lt. Aaron Van Zant, a Chinook helicopter pilot serving with the California Army National Guard, checks the right rear landing gear of his helicopter before the opening of the Western Air and Space Show at Vandenberg Air Force Base, California, on 31 October 2004. Some of the access panels on the sponson are open or removed.

An Army MH-47 hovers above Navy F/A-18 Hornets parked on the flight deck of USS *Kitty Hawk.* The Chinook is preparing to land on the flight deck as part of an approach-training and carrier-qualification program conducted in conjunction with the U.S. Navy.

Conspicuous among the gray Navy aircraft, a U.S. Army MH-47 Special Operations Force helicopter, deployed from Okinawa, is secured to the flight deck of USS *Kitty Hawk* (CV-63) as part of the aircrew's carrier qualifications in November 2002.

In a dramatic overhead view revealing rarely seen details of the top of a CH-47D Chinook, the crew is preparing to unload cargo at a landing zone during a relief operation to assist victims of a severe earthquake in northern Pakistan on 12 October 2005.

Marines hook a slingload of food supplies to a U.S. Army CH-47 during a relief operation in Pakistan on 27 February 2006. An Army aircrewman in the center cargo-hook hatch – commonly called the "hell hole" – is assisting the Marines in the operation.

In a view of the left side of the forward part of a Chinook, Brig. Gen. Andrew W. O'Donnell Jr., commanding general of the 3rd Marine Aircraft Wing (Forward), is in the copilot's seat, on 8 June 2010. In the window to the right is an M134 Minigun mount. (DVIDS)

In Afghanistan on 8 June 2010, Sgt. Maj. Anthony Spadaro, 3rd Marine Aircraft Wing (Forward), is being briefed on operating a window-mounted M134 Minigun in a CH-47 Chinook. The gunner could select a 2,000- or 4,000-round-per-minute rate of fire. (DVIDS)

Pakistanis sit on the floor of a U.S. Army CH-47 Chinook helicopter during an evacuation mission from Khyber Pakhtûnkhwâ, Pakistan, on 4 August 2010. The versatility of the Chinook is especially evident in relief missions such as this, when supplies are brought in and refugees flown out. (Department of Defense)

Two men hunker down and look away to protect themselves from rotor wash as a Nevada National Guard CH-47 lifts off with a Humvee slung underneath it during a training exercise at Nellis Air Force Base, Nevada, on 15 April 2011. (Department of Defense)

Pakistani civilians unload relief supplies delivered by a U.S. Army CH-47 from the 16th Combat Aviation Brigade in Swât Valley, Pakistan, on 3 November 2010. The two ramp extensions are attached to the rear of the ramp. (Department of Defense)

U.S. Marines from Delta Company, Anti-Terrorism Battalion, 4th Marine Division, and members of the Botswana Defense Force disembark from a Hawaii Army National Guard CH-47F during Exercise Southern Accord in Botswana on 3 August 2012. (Department of Defense)

Members of the 1st Battalion, 75th Ranger Regiment, rappel from an MH-47 during a combined-arms live-fire exercise near Fort Stewart, Georgia, on 10 January 2012. The MH-47's refueling probe and rescue lift are visible. (Department of Defense)

Army scouts board a Georgia Army National Guard CH-47, bound for the first Gainey Cup "Best Scout" competition at Fort Benning on 5 March 2013. The sign on the ramp reads "TEAM SAV." "085 GEORGIA" is on the rear of the pylon. (Department of Defense)

A soldier standing atop an M777A2 howitzer prepares to lift a sling hook up to a CH-47 from Task Force Knighthawk at Forward Operating Base Hadrian in Afghanistan on 18 June 2013. The howitzer was to be airlifted to Kandahâr Airfield. (Department of Defense)

U.S., Australian, and Chinese military personnel deplane from an Australian Army CH-47 at a remote landing zone in Northern Territory, Australia, on 12 October 2014, to conduct survival training as part of multinational exercise Kowari 2014. (Department of Defense)

Members of Team Dover and the 337th Airlift Squadron, Westover Air Reserve Base, Massachusetts, load the tail rotor pylon of a CH-47F, one of two Chinooks being delivered to Australia, into a C-5B Galaxy at Dover Air Force Base, Delaware, on 27 March 2015. (U.S. Air Force)

In a photo related to the preceding one, the fuselage of a CH-47F is about to be loaded into a C-5B from the 439th Airlift Wing, Westover Air Reserve Base, at Dover Air Force Base on 27 March 2015. The Australian Army had purchased two CH-47Fs, including this one. (U.S. Air Force)

The fuselage of a CH-47F is hauled, tail first, into the cargo hold of a C-5B Galaxy from the 439th Airlift Wing at Dover Air Force Base. With the rotor pylons removed, the fuselages of the CH-47Fs could be loaded into the C-5B with relative ease. (U.S. Air Force)

The nose of the CH-47F is positioned inside the cargo hold of the C-5B Galaxy, below the cockpit of the big transport jet. "ARMY" is stenciled in black on the nose of the Chinook. The side panels of the forward pylon are in place and are folded down. (U.S. Air Force)

A C-5M Super Galaxy has just delivered a CH-47 Chinook to Bagrâm Airfield, Afghanistan, on 26 December 2015. For transport in the C-5M, it was necessary to remove the Chinook's forward transmission gearbox and rotor assembly. (U.S. Air Force)

The rear rotor pylon of a Chinook helicopter is unloaded from a C-5M Super Galaxy at Bagrâm Airfield, Afghanistan, on 26 December 2015. When airlifting the CH-47, the rear rotor pylon was transported on the special dolly seen here. (U.S. Air Force)

U.S. Army pilot 1st Lt. T. J. Rose of 2-238th General Support Aviation Battalion Detachment 1, South Carolina Army National Guard, conducts preflight checks on a CH-47 at McEntire Joint National Guard Base, South Carolina, on 6 October 2015. (DVIDS)

A crewman washes the nozzle of the gas turbine engine of a CH-47 Chinook prior to an inspection at Bagrâm Airfield, Afghanistan, on 29 December 2015. This helicopter was a CH-47F, serial number 11-08830, marked for the Ohio Army National Guard. (DVIDS)

Two men from the 82nd Airborne Division Artillery strain to lift the sling rings to secure an M777A2 howitzer to a cargo hook on the belly of a hovering CH-47F Chinook assigned to 3rd General Support Aviation Battalion, during a field exercise at Fort Bragg, North Carolina, on 19 July 2016. The right pitot tube is the double-probe type that was a key exterior characteristic of the CH-47F. (DVIDS)

A soldier from Bravo Company, 2-238 General Support Aviation Battalion, South Carolina Army National Guard, refuels a CH-47 at McEntire Joint National Guard Base, South Carolina, during a statewide response to Hurricane Matthew in October 2016. (DVIDS)

A CH-47F from the 3rd General Support Aviation Battalion, 82nd Combat Aviation Brigade, lifts a sling-loaded M1114 Up-armored HMMWV during a training exercise at Fort Bragg. The HMMWV is well within the CH-47F's lift capacity of 21,000 pounds.

A CH-47 Chinook helicopter from Company B, 3-10 General Support Aviation Brigade, takes off during the 10th Mountain Division's annual Exercise Mountain Peak at Fort Drum, New York, in October 2016. (DVIDS)

A soldier adjusts the aft rotor pylon of CH-47F Chinook serial number 13-08149 at Hunter Army Airfield, Fort Stewart, Georgia, prior to a sling-load mission on 6 November 2016. Stenciled in yellow on the rotor blade is its serial number. (DVIDS)

South Carolina Army National Guard CH-47 pilots fly in support of the South Carolina Forestry Commission to fight a remote wildfire in the mountains in Pickens County, South Carolina, on 17 November 2016. (DVIDS)

Air National Guardsmen from Alaska and California unload search-and-rescue equipment from a CH-47 of the 2-149th General Support Aviation Battalion, Texas Army National Guard, in Orange, Texas, during Hurricane Harvey on 30 August 2017. (Staff Sgt. Balinda O'Neal Dresel/U.S. Army National Guard)

CH-47 crewmen of the 501st Aviation Regiment move a pallet of bottled water in the cargo compartment at JBSA-Randolph Auxiliary Airfield, Seguin, Texas, on 3 September 2017, in support of relief efforts in advance of Hurricane Harvey. (Tech. Sgt. Chad Chisholm/USAF)

To help airlift feed to livestock stranded by flood waters in the aftermath of Hurricane Harvey, members of Company B, 3rd Battalion, 238th Regiment, Ohio National Guard, load hay into a CH-47 in Jefferson County, Texas, on 7 September 2017.

Personnel from the National Guards of Pennsylvania and Puerto Rico cooperate in unloading a pallet of supplies from a CH-47 for the relief of victims of Hurricane Maria in San Juan, Puerto Rico, on 7 October 2017. (Sgt. José Ahiram Días-Ramos/PRNG-PAO)

Two soldiers of the 3rd General Support Aviation Battalion, 25th Infantry Division, are on the top deck of a CH-47 Chinook to perform maintenance on the helicopter, parked on a flightline at Contingency Operating Base Speicher, Tikrît, Iraq, in 2016. Now, six decades after Boeing Vertol delivered the prototype YHC-1As to the Army, the CH-47 Chinooks are still proving their worth every day, around the world, and will likely do so well into the future. (DVIDS)